VIOLA CLEVELAND

ART OF ONLINE WRITING

The Ultimate Guide on the Best Writing Tips to
Make Your Writing Better, Learn Expert Advice and
Tips on How to Unlock Your Writing Prowess

Descrierea CIP a Bibliotecii Naţionale a României
VIOLA CLEVELAND
    ART OF ONLINE WRITING. The Ultimate Guide on the
Best Writing Tips to Make Your Writing Better, Learn Expert
Advice and Tips on How to Unlock Your Writing Prowess /
Viola Cleveland – Bucharest: Editura My Ebook, 2021
    ISBN

VIOLA CLEVELAND

ART OF ONLINE WRITING

The Ultimate Guide on the Best Writing Tips to Make Your Writing Better, Learn Expert Advice and Tips on How to Unlock Your Writing Prowess

My Ebook Publishing House
Bucharest, 2021

TABLE OF CONTENTS

INTRODUCTION

If we're going to be really honest about it, most people don't like writing. And even people who like to write find it very difficult to get started.

As a writer, I've done a lot of research on writing and other writers, and the statements above are absolutely true. A very famous, successful mystery writer (I think it was James Patterson) said that there's no such thing as writer's block - writers just don't like what they write.

Nevertheless, we all need content for our businesses as much as we ever did. Sure, there are more ways to display content than there used to be - YouTube, Facebook, Twitter, and so on, but everything still starts with content.

The short solution to problems you have with your writing is to just write anyway. Get it on the page. Don't worry about it. You can fix it all with proofreading and editing. But you can't fix what isn't there.

That's the first tip, a big one. All writers say the same thing - the famous ones, the rich ones, the prolific ones – if you're having trouble getting started, the secret to creating content is first to get it on the page.

The purpose of this ebook is to show you some of the best things out there today to help you create content and to show you some evergreen methods that will always be current because good writing demands them.

As a business owner who needs content, you can either write your own or outsource it. Each option presents its own problems and solutions. In this ebook you will learn some techniques to make your own writing more enjoyable or to pass on to your writers to increase their productivity.

You'll also learn (or receive a refresher course) about how to write in different venues like blogs, Facebook, LinkedIn, or Twitter. Last, you get the briefest review of the most common grammar, punctuation, and usage mistakes.

All in all, I hope you get some benefit from this look at Online Writing Today.

WEBSITE OR BLOG DESIGN

Your writing begins with your website before you write a word. If your site is too confusing, readers won't stay around to read what you write ...or to buy. So, let's take just a minute to talk about designing your site.

Whether you have a website or a blog is your choice. You might want to have both. They're more and more often being used interchangeably, but here's the difference.

A website is more formal and static. Corporations and organizations and other businesses use websites to present information and products to their visitors. Blogs are more informal. They are platforms where you let visitors know who you are, present your products, etc., and often interact with visitors through comments. Information on blogs changes more frequently in general. Because of this, visitors search them for new information and tips and they are indexed more often by Google than websites.

Today many internet marketers have blogs as a subdirectory of their websites. This way, there is less overall maintenance, and the blog and the website both benefit somewhat from increased traffic.

Website/Blog Design Tips

- Plan your site so that it is inviting and easy for your readers to get around in.
- Make it interesting and clutter free.
- Know your goals for the site from products to the people you want to attract. These should play a part in everything you do on the site.
- Content is the main reason visitors come to your blog/ site. Put your content high on your page and support it with links to other content or helpful sites.
- Make your blog title inviting and use an appealing image at the top.

CONTENT IS KING

I've never met anyone in internet marketing who wasn't intelligent, have you? Now, some of them might have some other problems, most of us do, but people who can put together a website or blog, choose products to sell, manage traffic, write posts and articles, and manage social media -- these are intelligent people!

So, why do so many (over 90%) fail?

It's true -- many of them quit before their business is completely up and running, but what about the others? Well, let's see.

Think about the people you've come across in the past in internet marketing, the ones who are no longer around. I'll bet that they fall into one of these categories:

• The products they offered didn't seem worth buying

- You've bought from them and weren't satisfied with their previous products

- Their presentation (email, WSO, etc.) was so bad, it turned you off

- You just couldn't relate to them/their products

- They bombarded you with so many offers; you (and others) came to believe that they must be in it just for the money.

It doesn't have to be that way. At the core of successful internet marketing is just one concept: **content plus connection**. All the content -- whether it's a post or an article, a product, something on Facebook, or even a tweet -- needs to add some real value to the visitor's/reader's/buyer's life. If it doesn't, they might visit or read or buy once, but they very likely won't be back. That's content.

Equally important is connection. If you don't fulfill your readers' needs, they won't come back to read your posts. If your writing is full of typos and grammatical errors, it will seem like you don't care enough to do it right. If you can't get the post right, why should readers feel that your products are of value?

Why should they believe you care about them? That's connection.

You are your brand, so everything you write or do represents you. People define you by your products and your presentation. And people can be forgiving, but they also have long memories.

Content/Connection Mindset

First, know yourself and know why you're in internet marketing. If you're in it for a quick buck, okay. At least you know it. That's probably all it will be. The days are gone when people bought anything they came across. There's too much competition.

Second, decide that your products will offer value - they won't be copies of products already on the market. Find something unique that makes them worth buying. Represent your brand - you - with excellence. Take a few minutes to make sure that everything that goes out with your name is free the best you can make it.

Third, know who your readers (buyers) are and learn how to communicate with them in a way they can relate to and lets them get to know you. In general, writing on the internet is conversational.

Finally, remember to pay attention to your stats. Follow up with blog comments and on Facebook and Twitter.

Some Tips on Content/Connection

There's so much information out there. So much hype, so much good stuff, so much trash. What people need is your best efforts presented to them in ways that they can understand. Be authentic and if you give your readers that consistently, they will come to know, like, and trust you, and they will be loyal.

Here are some tips on creating content and connecting with your readers. They are evergreen and also up to date at the time this is being written.

- Make sure your personality shines through in an informal, conversational way. Writing on the internet is not as formal as writing in other venues.

- Keep your readers and their needs in mind whenever you sit down to write.

- What you say is more important than how often you say something. It's better to offer valuable content two or four times a month than to blog less valuable content more often.

- Make it clear to the reader that you're offering value by stating the problem clearly and offering a clear solution.

- Journal. You can keep ideas, tips, and information in it when you need ideas for posts.

- Always edit before posting to catch errors and take out unnecessary words.

- Read other bloggers, especially ones you admire. You might be able to learn a lot from them.

- Use contractions such as I'm and you'll to help keep a conversational tone.

- Same idea with starting sentences with "And" and "But." It's conversational.

- Ask questions. It's another great way to keep your reader involved.

- Keep current on what's going on by visiting blogs and forums.

- Stay clean and simple. Use one main idea per paragraph.

- Keep the attention on the topic. A little information about you is interesting to the reader, but you should not be the main event.

- Understand who your reader is before you start writing.

BRAINSTORMING

An Unconventional Approach that Works

Good brainstorming is basically unconventional thinking that works. The truth is that most of us have a hard time with it since all thinking, in school and in society, teaches us to follow the rules and think inside the box.

To make matters worse, when we do have unconventional ideas, we are the first ones to tell ourselves that they won't work.

Okay, since we know that now, we can go ahead and make a choice to think unconventionally anyway. No judgment. No brakes.

Let's take a look at how artists brainstorm. For one thing, they start with the material and subtract whatever doesn't belong. Along the way, they frequently adjust their focus or reframe what they see in their mind so that the finished sculpture isn't what they had in mind in the first place; it's better, more interesting.

Something that writers and copywriters do to come up with new ideas is put two conventional ideas together to come out with a new idea.

You can brainstorm by combining two conventional ideas, too. For instance,

- People are always trying to diet.
- People love chocolate.
- How about "Diet by Chocolate"?

It's completely doable since there are great substitutes for sugar and for high-fat dairy products that can be combined to produce low-calorie chocolate recipes.

This process will help you to brainstorm:

1. Think of a challenge to give yourself; for instance, a topic you'd like to write about.

2. You'll probably come up with conventional ideas first. Keep thinking.

3. Now the unconventional ideas will start coming. Entertain them, defend them, combine them.

Through this process you will probably glean your best ideas. That's how writers, musicians, and artists do it. As a matter of fact, cubism was invented by Pablo Picasso using this process when he was attempting to find a better way to paint portraits.

At the time, cubism was anti-conventional and extremely creative.

Highly creative people seem to follow this process naturally, but, as with a lot of other things, you can learn this process and get better at it with a little practice.

Tool for Brainstorming with Ease

The internet is a goldmine for brainstorming (you can first do the brainstorming and go back and use the same tools for researching your topics). Three of the most popular sources are Google, article directories, and forums.

Google Keyword Tracker

When you have some idea of what you want to write about, do some keyword research to see which words will be most profitable. You want some traffic but not a lot of competition. In other words, you want people searching for what you're writing about, but you don't want so much competition that it will be hard to sell to them.

Article Directory Research

Article directories like Ezinearticles.com are another goldmine for ideas. You'll find every topic along with variations and nuances. Don't steal their ideas; use them to jumpstart your own unique variations on a topic.

Forum Research

Forums are priceless for telling you what people care about. Whatever your topic is, search for forums related to it, then go in and see how their concerns can lead to ideas you want to write about.

When you have your list of ideas, a good way to come up with more ideas is to break the original ideas down into subtopics. For instance, we all need fiber, but getting enough fiber is different for the elderly than it is for the toddler, and different for the athlete than it is for the executive. It's different for the vegan than it is for carnivores. See, endless!

A great way to brainstorm is through the use of mindmaps. Let's take a look at mindmaps in the next chapter.

OUTLINES AND MINDMAPS

Two ways to shape your ideas into something you can write from are with outlines or with mindmaps. You might like writing with pen and paper or have other reasons why you use outlines, so I'll include that choice. Mindmaps are more flexible. You can use them for brainstorming and go on to turn those ideas into an outline on the same mindmap.

Outlines

Let's talk in terms of an article or a blog post. An acceptable size for these is about 500 words, and the standard outline will have five paragraphs consisting of an introduction, a body of three paragraphs, and a conclusion.

These are generalities, though. They are guidelines for you and not at all set in stone. All of these can vary depending on what you have to say in your piece. That's even more true since you're writing on the internet where varying your paragraphs with numbering and bullets and highlighting, etc. adds to your writing by making it interesting and easier on the eyes.

So, remember that this outline model is best used as an example of one way to build a post or article:

Post/Article Outline

Introduction

- Capture your reader's attention
- Introduce your general topic
- State your point of view about the topic

Three Paragraphs in Body

Each of these three paragraphs should concentrate on a different aspect of the main topic.

Each paragraph should have a thesis statement, stating the idea of the paragraph. The rest of the paragraph should support that statement with statistics, stories, quotations, or supporting ideas.

Create transitions between paragraphs so that the ideas flow logically from one to the next. One way to do this is with bridge phrases like

- on the other hand

- another example is

Conclusion

An effective conclusion ties up what you've said, and when it's well written, it leaves the reader with something to remember.

Mindmaps

Xmind is software that allows you to organize your ideas and reorganize them as you go along. You can get the software free at www.xmind.net. You can use xmind for things like product creation, webinars, ebooks, etc., but here we'll use it to organize ideas for a blog post.

The topic is Healthy Eating, with ideas for an introduction, three paragraphs in the body, and a conclusion.

Healthy Eating

Introduction
Lots of Choices Easy to do

Fiber

Complex Carbohydrates

More Good Carbs available now

Fruits and vegetables Farmers Markets Buy in season Freeze for all year

High quality protein Fish and chicken Lean beef Protein shakes

Conclusion

Feel so good! Look so good!

With a mindmap, you can add topics and subtopics, move them around, or delete them on the screen easily. Mindmaps are flexible and easy to use.

EDITING AND PROOFREADING

Proofreading is one of the easiest tasks in writing, but it's also one of the most essential. You don't want your work to look unprofessional due to avoidable errors that are easy to fix.

1. Spell Checking and Grammar Checking

Often these days we're writing on computers and using programs that have spell check and grammar check.

Absolutely, you should use them, but you should remember that they don't pick up everything. If a word is spelled correctly, the spell checker won't pick it up as the wrong word.

For instance, the spell checker won't see that

"They will meat later." should really be "They will meet later."

Unfortunately, grammar checkers miss many things as well. After all, they are machines and can't think the way you can. So, use the spell/grammar check and then go over the work one more time to look for any errors that the checkers missed.

2. Run-ons and Fragments

Run-on sentences and sentence fragments are two of the most common errors of new writers. Make sure that each clause is independent and can stand alone. Make sure that you don't combine two unrelated clauses into one sentence.

3. Verb–Subject Agreement

Check that you have the correct verb forms with your nouns. A very common problem in writing is pairing singular verbs with plural nouns and vice versa. It becomes more confusing when there are words between the noun and the verb.

4. Misspelling Confusing Words

It's easy to fly right by words that are spelled correctly but are the wrong words when you are proofreading too quickly. Look out especially for the most common problem words:
your/you're they're/their/there affect/effect advise/advice lie/lay sit/set

5. Punctuation and Capitalization Errors

These errors are also easy to miss if you don't take the time to proofread. Remember,

- every sentence begins with a capital letter
- every sentence ends with a period (or other end mark)
- check for comma errors
- include apostrophes with possessive nouns

Some Editing and Proofreading Tips

1. Take a break, if possible, between writing your document and proofreading it. It will help you look at it more objectively.

2. Read your document out loud. This will help you catch many errors. It will also help you to find better ways to express some of things you've written.

3. Slow down. Read your document carefully and slowly. Look at it as if someone else wrote it and you are seeing it for the first time.

4. Print out your document and mark the errors with a pen. Often, it's easier to see them on a printed copy.

5. Once you know the rules, break them once in a while for emphasis. For instance, it's okay to use a sentence fragment when it's clearly being used for emphasis...and not a mistake on your part.

6. If you don't use an outline or a mindmap to put your ideas in logical order before you write, editing is even more important for you. Read what you wrote to make sure it is said in the best order possible and with support for each idea.

7. If you use a recording device like Dragon Speaking Naturally, look for the words that are misunderstood and left out.

8. If you're having a hard time concentrating, walk away if at all possible and come back to it.

9. Don't forget to check for the "know, like, and trust" factor. Will your readers know, like, and trust you after they read this piece?

BLOGGING FOR YOUR BUSINESS

Has this ever occurred to you? Your blog is another form of social media...but one you have lots of control over!

The Benefits of Blogging

A business blog is an asset to corporate bloggers and individual entrepreneurs alike. It's a source of low-cost, highly targeted leads, a showcase for your expertise, an opportunity to build relationships with your customers, and a magnet for traffic to your website. Wow!

• Like social media, your blog lets you connect with your customers in a more personal way. It's interactive. It makes you a living human being instead of static website. People can get to know you and begin to know, like and trust you.

- Your blog gives you a chance to demonstrate your expertise and establish your credibility. This is where you show your customers what you know with your posts.

And since your posts change frequently, this will build your credibility.

- Through your blog, you have the most cost-effective marketing at your fingertips. It combines low-cost marketing and promotion of your products with a way to get information on your target market through their comments and your stats.

- If you have a website, writing as little as one post a week on your blog will increase your standing in the search engines. If you SEO your posts, you'll climb higher and faster.

As you can see, successful blogging is a bit art and a bit science. One way to gain valuable insight into it is by listening to already successful bloggers.

In The Secret to Making Money with Your Blog, Nicole Dean recorded interviews with several successful bloggers and is kind enough to share them. Nicole asked them all one question, "How do you personally make money with your blog or blogs?"

Lain Ehmann's advice: The key to making money through your blog is to KNOW YOUR AUDIENCE. She currently has streams of income making money in

-Affiliate sales

-Information products

-Online courses

-Live events

-Sponsored posts

-Adsense

-CPA campaigns

-Continuity programs

Still, her advice is to focus your efforts - maximize your efforts with one thing before moving on to another. Then keep building.

Susanne Myer's advice: She uses her blog for two main purposes: building her list and making product recommendations. She tailors her content to the interests of the visitors to each blog. For instance, on her blog for affiliate marketers, she only discusses affiliate marketing. First, she concentrates on getting visitors to join her list. Then, she monetizes by offering affiliate and her own products.

Shannon Cherry's advice: Shannon's approach to her many blogs is that they make money or they're gone. She monetizes with links to her products and services in posts and with affiliate links. She also hosts press releases and announces product and service launches. She makes it a point to monetize all her posts with links and calls to action. Her advice is to love blogging, provide a service, but monetize everything.

Nicole Dean's advice: Nicole agrees with each person interviewed. She provides valuable information but monetizes everything with links to products. She repurposes her content. For instance, these interviews are blog posts but will also be turned into a book. She builds her list but also asks her list to share her information and product links. Her advice is to ask your readers what they want you to do for them. You can't read their minds.

10 Most Excellent Blogging Tips

Some of these tips have been alluded to before, but they're so spot on they need to be mentioned explicitly.

1. Be clear about what your readers are to do. Give clear calls to action in each blog post. Give clear action steps if

needed, tell them to sign up for your newsletter, and explicitly ask them to snare your posts.

2.   Promote, promote, promote. Get the news out there in every way you can: optimize your blog, announce your posts, and connect with other bloggers.

3.   Pay attention to your customers. Don't let your blog lie there, update it and make a commitment to it for the long term.

4.   Monitor your comments. It's a great connection with your customers. Comments make you seem friendly, and they build trust.

5.   Write suck-you-in headlines for your posts. Grab readers' attention and make them curious to learn more about what you have to say.

6.   Share. Share your content every way you can and with everyone. You're not giving away information for free because valuable free information will keep your readers coming back.

7.   Put buttons on your blog. Use every share button you can

- Facebook "Like" buttons, Twitter and Pinterest buttons, etc.

8.   Use more than text. A great thing about blogging is that it's so easy to incorporate all sorts of videos, images, etc. Your readers will appreciate it and share them.

9. Give comment love. Encourage your readers to comment and always reply.

10. Remember - your blog is a business. Maintain it. Make a schedule to blog. Check comments and stats to know how you're doing.

Top 10 Grammar and Punctuation Mistakes

Grammar and punctuation mistakes can make your writing seem uneducated and careless, but correcting those mistakes is not that difficult if you keep these rules in mind.

It might not be a surprise to you that comma errors are at the top of the top of the "Mistakes" list (along with misuse of "tricky" words).

1. **Commas separating independent clauses**

When two independent clauses are joined by a coordinating conjunction (and, or, nor, for, so, yet, but), you need a comma:

- Sally went to school, and her father went to work.
- Jesse didn't feel well, so he stayed home.

2. Commas separating dependent and independent clauses

When a dependent clause precedes an independent clause, you need a comma:

- If I leave work early today, I can get to the matinee.

When a dependent clause comes after an independent clause, you don't need a comma:

- I can get to the matinee if I leave work early today.

3. Commas separating introductory words or phrases

An introductory phrase or group of words needs a comma unless it's very short.

- On second thought, let's get pizza.
- Tonight we'll order pizza.

4. Sentence fragments

Every complete sentence requires a subject and a verb. Sentence fragments lack one or the other.

- Home on the range. (no verb)
- Ate some chicken for lunch. (no subject)

5. Verb–subject agreement

Subjects and verbs must agree in person and number. This can be confusing when the subject and verb are separated by a group of words:

- <u>Kylie</u>, the girl in the orange dress and sneakers, <u>is</u> a junior.

- <u>People</u> who are intelligent often <u>enjoy</u> playing chess.

6. Colons and semi-colons

Colons introduce lists or specific definitions:

- Please buy these things at the store: matches, light bulbs, and cottage cheese.

Semi-colons separate clauses that are closely related:

- We take the same classes in school; we both love biology.

7. Repeated subjects or objects

Other languages allow a subject or object to be repeated in its own clause, but English doesn't allow this. In other languages, this is correct:

- The <u>purse</u> that had been stolen <u>it</u> was found.

In English the correct sentence must be

- The purse that had been stolen was found.

The same is true for objects: Incorrect:

- The little dog chased the <u>car</u> that his owner was riding in <u>it</u>.

Correct:

- The little dog chased the car that his owner was riding in.

8. **Parallelism**

Items in a series should be the same. When your using nouns, verbs, adjectives, etc. in a series, they should all agree.

Incorrect:

- Sam loves skiing, running track, and basketball.

Correct:

- Sam loves skiing, running track, and playing basketball.

9. Apostrophes

Many nouns and pronouns add s to form the plural and 's to show possession. It versus it's is a very good example since lots of people make a mistake with this pronoun.

- It's means It is - It is a beautiful day.

- Its means ownership - The computer was left on the bus by its owner.

10. Quotation Marks

Quotation marks indicate direct quotations or exact statements of others. Indirect statements, or making reference to what someone said doesn't require quotation marks.

- Mom told Dad, "Please come home early from work tonight."

- Mom asked Dad if he would please come home early from work tonight.

TOP 10 TRICKY WORDS

Some words in the English language cause more problems than others.

These ten sets of words are at the top of the list of troublesome words, but there are plenty more. The best thing to do if you are at all unsure is to look the word up.

1. Among/Between

- Among is used with three entities
- Between is used with two entities

The lottery was divided among several winners. Choose between waffles and pancakes.

2. Bad/Badly

- Bad is an adjective describing a noun

- Badly is an adverb

The boy was bad.

The boy was badly hurt by the fly ball.

3. Bring/Take

- Bring means an object is being carried toward you.

- Take means an object is being carried away from you.

Please bring me that book.

Please take these files to your desk.

4. Choose/Chose

- Choose is a verb meaning "select."

- Chose is the past tense of choose, meaning "selected."

Susan chose an ivory dress for her wedding.

You should choose the option that works best for you.

5. Fewer/Less

- Fewer refers to items that can be counted

- Less refers to uncountable amounts

Fewer people are in the middle class today. Less sugar would make this a healthier drink.

6. Good/Well

- Good is an adjective
- Well is an adverb

She's a good girl.

She is feeling well today after being sick for a long time.

7. Loose/Lose

- Loose is an adjective meaning "not tight."
- Lose is a verb meaning either "to misplace" or "not to win." Did you lose the dog, or did he get loose from his leash?

8. Their/There/They're

- Their is a possessive adjective meaning "belonging to them."
- There is an adverb referring to a location of something or someone.
- They're is a shortened form of they are.

They're in the waiting room to pick up their children. You can find them there.

9. Two/To/Too

- Two is a number
- To is a preposition
- Too is an adverb

You two boys are going to the cafeteria for breaks too many times.

10. Whose/Who's

- Whose is a possessive pronoun.
- Who's is a contraction of who is.

Whose hat is this? Who's going home now?

ONLINE WRITING TIPS

Facebook

Do you know anyone who's not on Facebook? Probably not very many people, anyway. The biggest companies and the most successful business people all over the world are on Facebook. Why?

Because they see its tremendous power - 24/7 - to build relationships with millions of people anywhere in the world...and on autopilot. That's the potential for making lots and lots of money, given the right formula.

Facebook Tips That Work

Messages you leave on Facebook can increase your success or detract from it. These tips should help.

• Develop your style - Keep your writing style in messages appropriate to Facebook. That means, informal and social, personal and appropriate. No heavy negativity or heavy sales pitch, either. You might want to write similar to the way you speak.

- Keep it short and focused on the main point - Respect other people's time and stay on message.

- Give valuable information of interest - Giving people something they want or need by way of information is a way to start building a relationship.

When it comes to Facebook fan pages (where you post your products), these tips on posts might come in handy.

- Write posts relevant to the topic of the fan page.

- Post questions and start discussions relevant to your target audience to encourage responses.

- Analyze your posts. Look at the responses and likes you're getting. Are you missing the mark? Do your readers want something you're not providing?

Pinpointing these issues will pay off in the future.

Five things never to do on Facebook

1. Never spam. You want to promote and engage equally. No one wants to see posts full of links.

2. Keep you personal and professional pages separate. Combining them can confuse the reader and cause mistrust.

3. Never attack people. You won't please everyone. Just ignore the criticism and move past it. Or delete it.

4. Don't leave your fans stranded. The main point of social media is interaction. It makes you human.

5. Have a plan. What do you want to accomplish? If you don't know, you won't accomplish it.

LinkedIn

LinkedIn has a big problem -- that's good! Most people still think of LinkedIn as ineffective for producing results in internet marketing. But the problem is not with LinkedIn; the problem is with the way internet marketers are approaching it.

As you probably know, LinkedIn is the largest professional network in the world. It's a place where professionals connect with each other and build a network of solid long-term relationships. These relationships can result in enormous sales of products and services, eventually. But it's all in the approach.

Tips for Presenting Yourself on LinkedIn

How you present yourself is very important on LinkedIn. It takes pride in distinguishing itself as a business site, so the informal atmosphere and approach encountered on Facebook or a blog is unacceptable. If you're unfamiliar with LinkedIn, you can learn more about the "rules" on many paid and free sources. Here we'll discuss how to best present yourself.

PROFILE

Your first chance to put your best face forward is on your profile. Your profile speaks for you. It's your first impression.

- PHOTO - Have a professional looking photo. No party hats here. You want people to use your services or buy your products, so look your best.

- YOUR URL - LinkedIn assigns you a non-descript url by default. Edit this to use your own name if it's available. That way, people will find you more easily.

- PROFESSIONAL HEADLINE - The keywords you want to be associated with should be in your headline. Searches are done on LinkedIn by scanning the keywords in each profile headline.

- ACCURATE, ENGAGING SUMMARY - Your summary captures your entire career in few words. Make it stand out by answering prospective clients' needs. Use keywords here as well.

- ACCOMPLISHMENTS - Be accurate and specific about your accomplishments. Be relevant and quantify your accomplishments if possible.

Make your profile as interesting as possible. In your case you are probably not applying for a job, so let people know who you are, what area(s) you work in, what products or services you offer, and what things make you stand out.

When you've completed your profile, don't walk away and hope for the best. There's a protocol to follow to make yourself known in LinkedIn. You need to be assertive in order to be found, but in the way LinkedIn defines, which is different from anywhere else.

Be sure you follow up with

- Building your contacts - Connect with past and present colleagues and alumni.

- Cultivating and using recommendations -

Recommendations are powerful because they are authentic, so trusted in LinkedIn more than in other venues.

- Using groups - Groups can be of help to you in three ways: they can help develop your profile, assist with lead generation, and aid in your own personal development.

• Promoting your events - Promotion is easy in LinkedIn once you have established yourself because the right groups are easily targeted with the result that your information can be quickly spread and your brand recognition will spread.

• Using status updates - Status updates are underused in LinkedIn. Update your profile with relevant blog posts and other news items.

If you follow LinkedIn's guidelines, there's enormous potential for success.

Twitter

Twitter is an outrageously successful social media platform that you no doubt already are somewhat familiar with.

Basically, you have up to 140 characters per tweet to announce anything you want to.

As an online entrepreneur, your general goals with Twitter are to generate as large a following as possible, to retain those followers, and to engage them so that they buy your products and services. If you're really good, your followers might retweet your message (send it to their Twitter friends) or even be "favorited," which will make you very popular.

So, the question is, "What do you have to do to create messages in 140 characters that are so intriguing that your followers and potential customers will click your link?"

Tips for Great Tweets

Your tweets must interest the person reading them; that means that they must be personal and be about things that interest the reader. Furthermore, what you really want is not just for the reader to click on your link, but also to share, like, recommend, tweet and forward your information and link. To accomplish this, you need to ask yourself some questions.

What do you want your tweets to say about you and your brand? How can you make this "statement" appealing the people following you?

You need a sound knowledge of the value of your information, your brand, and your product or service. Your tweets act as spurts of information that capture the reader's attention and imagination.

What appeals to your readers? What content are they looking for?

Once you know this, you can begin to determine what information they want to get and how they want it presented.

You can decide what to include in the recommendations, requests, questions, answers, invitations, and offers you send to them.

Try some of these tips:

1. Engage your audience emotionally by asking a question or suggesting that they do something.

2. Respond to every tweet you receive; you never know where it might lead.

3. Provide valuable, relevant information to your base. Credit the source if there is one.

4. Be truthful. Don't lie in order to get people to click on your link. You'll pay for it later.

5. Be brief. Keep your tweet focused on one point.

6. Don't "flood" your base with tweets. Be considerate and space out your tweets.

One way to think of your tweet is as if it were a headline. Create a question of some kind in the reader's mind so that he wants to click the link to get more information. Be sure to leave a link. Use interesting terms or pop culture items or breaking news your readers can relate to. Choose something that will grab them and keep them.

CONCLUSION

To sum up, have a good time with writing content in all its forms. Let your personality shine through -- readers like that and connect with it. Make it a conversation that speaks to your readers as if they are friends you care about.

At the same time, remember to give value by taking the time to make your content unique in some way. Show your readers that you respect them by

- Making your writing correct. If you don't remember the rules for punctuation, grammar, and word usage, brush up on them.

- Having a plan for what you want to say. Don't ramble or repeat yourself. It bores your readers and disrespects their time.

- Presenting your ideas clearly. Simplicity is better than complexity, even when you're presenting complex ideas.

Finally, remember that you are writing for your business. Your ultimate goal is to make money. Relate your writing to products of value that your turn your readers to buyers.

Printed by Libri Plureos GmbH in Hamburg,
Germany